AT HOME
ON THE
WATER

AT HOME
ON THE
WATER

JACI CONRY

GIBBS SMITH
TO ENRICH AND INSPIRE HUMANKIND

First Edition
26 25 24 23 22   5 4 3 2 1

Text © 2022 Jaci Conry
Photographs by Donna Dotan: pages 157–175, 207
Photographs by Greg Premru: pages 188–205
Photographs by Jane Beiles: pages 5, 6, 8, 17–41, 106–117
Photographs by Jared Kuzia: pages 86–105 and back cover
Photographs by Jessica Glynn: pages 12, 71–85, 176–187, and front cover
Photographs by Julie Soefer: pages 3, 10–11, 134–155, 208
Photographs by Karen Millet: pages 15, 56–69, 119–133
Photographs by Stacy Zarin Goldberg: pages 14, 43–54

Published by
Gibbs Smith
P.O. Box 667
Layton, Utah 84041

1.800.835.4993 orders
www.gibbs-smith.com

Designed by Ryan Thomann and Virginia Snow
Printed and bound in China

Gibbs Smith books are printed on either recycled, 100% post-consumer waste, FSC-certified papers or on paper produced from sustainable PEFC-certified forest/controlled wood source. Learn more at www.pefc.org.

Library of Congress Cataloging-in-Publication Data

Names: Conry, Jaci, author.
Title: At home on the water / Jaci Conry.
Description: First edition. | Layton, Utah : Gibbs Smith, [2022]
Identifiers: LCCN 2021022853 | ISBN 9781423657507 (hardcover) | ISBN 9781423657514 (epub)
Subjects: LCSH: Seaside architecture—United States. | Second homes—United States. | Vacation homes—United States.
Classification: LCC NA7575 .C65 2021 | DDC 728.70973—dc23
LC record available at https://lccn.loc.gov/2021022853

For Mike, Max, and Emma: Anywhere you are is home to me

CONTENTS

INTRODUCTION

My husband's parents have a summer home on Cape Cod. Perched on a small bluff overlooking Buzzards Bay, the house has a sloped, rocky pathway that leads down to the beach. The shingle-clad house is a rambling structure, four bedrooms aligned on one level, each one with a view of the ocean. It is a home from which to observe so many things: shorebirds and seals on the wide, flat rocks of the jetty; sailboats and fishermen; the ocean's multitude of hues. There's subtle and, occasionally, not so subtle drama to be witnessed when the ever-changing skyline meets the sea. Sunsets and sunrises and storms take on great significance there. Scents are heightened: the whiff of marine life, salty water and sunscreen, and the beach roses that grow wild all around permeates the air.

A house by the sea conjures magical notions of an oasis. At the mention of one, we imagine a place geared for relaxation and outdoor living, a place for wiling away afternoons with a book. At that dreamy beach house, there will be picnics and sea-glass collecting; togetherness and bathing suits; lemonade and seafood; laughter and cocktails at sunset (or much earlier); and sand, sand everywhere. That's what a house on the water means.

In my career as a design writer, I've visited countless ocean havens. Truly, they come in all shapes and sizes. From the most rustic of cottages, with century-old board-and-batten paneling, no-fuss furniture, and antique hooked rugs, their colors long faded to sleek-lined, white minimalist manses with walls of glass and state-of-the-art smart-home systems. In all cases, these homes by the sea are much beloved by their inhabitants. They are places to which people come home again and again when they're in need of ease and serenity, breaks from lives of busyness.

And when did this fascination with homes by the water arise? When did white sand and rolling waves become symbolic of leisure time? The practice of taking respite in oceanside locales originated among the European elite who began touting the curative qualities of fresh air, exercise, and sea bathing as early as the mid-eighteenth century. As

Britain embraced the Industrial Revolution, those who labored in the country's increasing number of factories were viewed as having stronger and more resilient constitutions. The upper classes, long considered fragile, sought to improve their physical prowess, and the notion of the ocean having a restorative nature emerged. Along England's eastern shore, coastal resort communities catered to a growing clientele of wellness seekers who sought the sea's treatment for a variety of conditions, including melancholy, gout, tubercular infections, leprosy, and hysteria.

It was called "sea bathing" back in the late 1700s, and by the turn of the next century, the practice of swimming in the ocean was mainstream for those seeking a cure for any type of ailment. Those so dedicated to the healing properties of time spent by the sea built their homes in coastal European enclaves. As the 1800s progressed, romantic sensibilities began to be attached to the ocean. "It was Romantic

ABOVE: This casual seating area features tones that evoke the coastal locale—including a rug in alternating sand-colored hues and blue throws and pillows—in an understated way. **OPPOSITE:** Steps lead down the sloped pathway to the pool area of this Nantucket retreat.

writers and artists at the turn of the nineteenth century who added emotion and wonder to the act of strolling along the beach or watching the tide turn," writes Daniela Blei, in a *Smithsonian Magazine* article titled "Inventing the Beach: The Unnatural History of a Natural Place." The coastal landscape became "a site of transformative experience, where the individual was immersed in nature. . . . The beach held the promise of self-discovery."

According to Alain Corbin, a professor at Paris's Sorbonne University and author of *The Lure of the Sea: The Discovery of the Seaside in the Western World*, by the 1840s, the beach had become a sought-after escape from the city and the drudgery of modern life for many Europeans. There was an "irresistible awakening of a collective desire for the shore," he explains. The rail system made train travel affordable and easy, which resulted in middle-class families taking to the shore in increasing numbers. Vacation, which had once meant an involuntary absence from work, became a desired interlude that people looked forward to all year long.

Over the course of the 1800s, the phenomenon of the seaside resort made its way to France, Italy, and Germany. Eventually, the appeal of coastal havens took hold across the Atlantic in the United States. As the great wealth from the post-Civil War boom created the Gilded Age, the country's wealthiest families built palatial seaside homes in Newport, Rhode Island, and Palm Beach, Florida. As time went on, other elite private retreats flourished on Cape Cod and in California's coastal enclaves.

In the early decades of the 1900s, as American industry boomed, the rise of the automobile revolutionized landscapes and lifestyles. More middle-class families found themselves with cars and a little extra cash. Craving time outside and a reprieve from their frenetic lifestyles, they took to the coastlines of this country to build homes where they could spend extended periods of time—the entire summer, if circumstances allowed—together.

The rest is, as they say, history. The concept of a "beach house" is ingrained in American lexicon. It is idealized and celebrated. On these pages, you will find a wide range of residences, all located by the sea, throughout the United States. They vary widely in architecture and aesthetic—from a glamorous Spanish-style 1920s manse in Palm Beach to a tucked-away, weathered-grey Nantucket cottage decorated with artful collectibles to a white-and-glass marvel designed by a renowned Modernist in Connecticut to a chic retreat located amid the activity on the Strand in Hermosa Beach, California. Despite their differences, the homes are similar in concept. These are homes meant for relaxation, for enjoying life, for being with others and getting back to basics. These are structures that enable healing from the stressors of schedules, meant for enjoying the view and for letting in nature and its nourishing affects. They are cherished homes, much beloved by the folks who live in them, families who graciously shared them with me and the much larger audience of this book.

I hope you enjoy each one as much I did.

—Jaci Conry

TOP OPPOSITE: In a Hyannis Port home, the family room's wall of glass affords maximum views of the beach; the blues of the ocean and sky are reflected in the room's textiles, while sand tones are found in the sisal carpet and the coffee table. **BOTTOM OPPOSITE:** In the adjacent dining room, half of the beadboard-clad walls are painted white, while the upper portion is a deep blue.

OPPOSITE: Custom-painted oars reflect colors of personal significance to the family who lives in this Ocean City house. **ABOVE:** To give the white expanse distinction, designer Marie Flanigan had shiplap paneling installed on the base of the kitchen island.

DIAMOND IN THE ROUGH

PHOTOGRAPHY BY JANE BEILES

S ituated at the end of a long, sandy drive, this secluded home has direct access to a beach that few people are aware exists. On Nantucket, homes with such close access to the ocean are scarce, and when the homeowners discovered this property was for sale two decades ago, they felt unbelievably lucky.

At the time the homeowners purchased the property, there were two structures on-site: a long, rectangular beach cottage that wasn't winterized and a tiny square shedlike building with baseboard heating. Nantucket's rigid building codes—designed to ensure that the island's historic architecture is preserved—stipulated that the structures could be renovated, but they had to stay within the original footprint. Fortunately, to gain space, the homeowners were able to add a second story to the two-bedroom cottage, doubling the home's square footage.

Hallmarks of coastal New England's historic cottage-style architecture abound, including walls paneled with shiplap and wainscotting. On the main level, the original ceiling beams remain exposed,

infusing the rooms with volume, distinction, and a sense of nostalgia.

Clad on the exterior with cedar shingles that weather with each passing year and topped with a cedar-shake roof, the house is a summer retreat for the family, which now includes grandchildren. "Our son lives in Nashville and our daughter is in Chicago with her three children," says the wife. "Every summer we all spend time together at the house. It's a special place for us."

The homeowners are antiques enthusiasts, and the place is filled with cherished furniture and accents. After their children had grown up, the couple tapped Michelle Holland of Nantucket House Antiques & Interior Design Studio to help revamp the home's aesthetic. "When you have so many special pieces like they do, it can be hard to know where to put things," says Holland. "We focused on displaying their collectibles in an order where they can be appreciated."

An assemblage of doorstops fashioned as sailors, for example, are now arranged in the living

The house is filled with decorative objects, including this wall-mounted green clock and a sailor's valentine crafted of countless tiny shells.

room's built-in shelves, on which a series of rattan and wood Nantucket lightship baskets woven by the wife's father in the 1980s also hold a place of prominence. Maritime art in a range of styles, including impressionistic, folk art, and hand carvings, pay homage to Nantucket's nautical roots. Other elements nod to the coastal locale in an understated and occasionally whimsical way, including a series of plates festooned with lobsters. Brass ship lights and other antique lighting, including gas fixtures in the foyer that Holland had electrified, provide both illumination and a timeless sense of place.

While a house filled with antiques is not always considered comfortable, the homeowners strove to ensure that theirs is a relaxing haven. "This is a family home first and foremost, and the main objective was that it be comfortable," says Holland. Upholstered furniture provides plenty of space to lounge, and hooked rugs that the wife passionately collects feel soft underfoot, due to their decades of use.

In the living room, a square table where the grandchildren play games—sometimes with their parents and grandparents—is nestled up close to a window overlooking the vast swath of beach and ocean, which provides the stunning backdrop to their life at the house. "Even when we're not outside," says the wife, "we're always appreciating the setting."

OPPOSITE: Nestled in the dunes, the house is privileged to have direct access to a private beach. **ABOVE:** The new stair runner had to have a "hand-done look for it to work with all of the antique rugs in the house," says designer Michelle Holland.

The living room's upholstered furniture is comfortable and casual, perfect for flopping on after a day at the beach. Since the house is in such a remote location, there are no window treatments, allowing maximum views of the sea.

ABOVE: The homeowners enjoy playing games at the antique game table with their grandchildren on rainy days. **OPPOSITE:** Built-in shelves showcase the couple's cherished collectibles and books.

OPPOSITE: In the second-floor hallway, a slim sofa is oriented toward a band of French doors and windows that overlook the ocean. **ABOVE:** The home's weathered-shingle exterior is unassuming and rustic, reminiscent of a time gone by.

MIDCENTURY MARVELOUS

PHOTOGRAPHY BY JANE BEILES

Pritzker Architecture Prize–winning architect Richard Meier was just thirty-one when he designed this home, the iconic Smith House, in Darien, Connecticut, in 1965. Meier, an acolyte of Bauhaus pioneer Marcel Breuer, would become known all over the world for his refinements of and variations on Modernist principles, but when he designed this home as a summer residence for Chuck Smith's parents, he was living in a two-room apartment, barely getting by. The design of this geometric three-story house, however, would ultimately propel Meier's career into the spotlight.

Chuck Smith and his brothers grew up spending summers at Smith House, and while it wasn't exactly geared for children, with its with stark white walls and a grid of glass overlooking Long Island Sound, he appreciated the architectural marvel's significance early on. "It was like living in a sculpture or piece of art," recalls Smith, noting that there has always been great interest in the house. "People—sometimes busloads of them—would come up the driveway trying to get a glimpse of it, and architectural students would come by wanting to study it. Our mother always welcomed those who were interested in taking a look at the house."

The property's sloping site makes for positively unrivaled water views. Because the land's foundation was almost entirely rock, Meier opted to extend the house vertically rather than horizontally to conserve excavation costs.

The street-facing side of the house, where visitors enter on the middle level, blurs with the scenery, appearing as an opaque white box pierced with small, dark-glass windows. Directly opposite the front door, the eye is drawn to a painted-brick fireplace that pushes to the outside through a tight frame of mullions. Suspended between the chimney and the steel structural columns, a massive, glazed wall focused on the arresting ocean view creates a shell encompassing the living spaces. "You don't see the view right away; you just notice the fireplace—and then you look to the right and left of it and see the glass, and it's a huge moment," says Smith. The

In the office, a built-in desk is oriented alongside a plate-glass window that overlooks the ocean.

whiteness of the home reflects and refracts the colors of nature in a way that it heightens one's perception of the landscape.

Meier, also an abstract artist and furniture designer, created several pieces for the home, including an elongated horizontal wall hanging fashioned out of interlocking cubes painted in primary colors, which remains in its original spot in the dining room more than fifty years after the house was built. There's also a sofa Meier designed on the third floor and a built-in desk between two walls of glass in the office. However, Smith admits there's not usually much work going on when he's there. "It's very hard to focus," he says. "You just are so drawn to the view; with all of the glass you want to see what's going on outside all the time."

ABOVE: Midcentury furnishings and a zebra-hide rug in a seating area tie into the origins of the home.
OPPOSITE: A cozy nook offers just enough space for an Eero Saarinen–inspired table.

A modern red sculpture infuses color into the all-white aesthetic that dominates not only the great room, but also most of the house.

ABOVE: Chuck Smith designed the origami-inspired wall hanging to infuse a burst of color into the dining room. **OPPOSITE:** The fireplace was built into the wall to integrate it seamlessly into the room.

The house was designed with outdoor areas on every level to offer ample opportunities to interact with the setting.

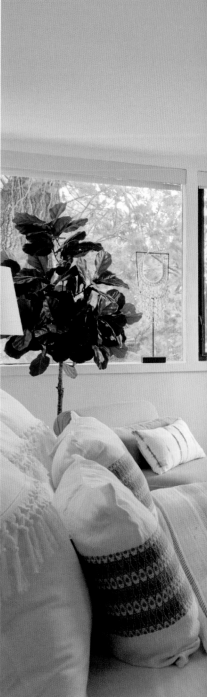

OPPOSITE: A built-in vanity is part of the primary suite. **ABOVE:** The bedrooms are compact spaces with small windows that look out on the tree-shrouded side of the house.

ABOVE and **TOP OPPOSITE:** Bold shades of orange and blue enliven a secondary bedroom.
BOTTOM OPPOSITE: Just big enough for a twin bed, these bedrooms were designed solely for sleeping, whereas the upper-level living spaces are vast and open.

ABOVE: A slightly larger bedroom accommodates a full-size bed and is jazzed up with Marimekko bedding. **RIGHT:** One of the glass panes used in the house is nearly three stories high and was delivered by boat and then heaved up the jetty to the homesite. As a child, Smith remembers his parents, who were fearful of breaking the glass, constantly telling him not to throw balls in the house.

ROOM FOR MORE

PHOTOGRAPHY BY STACY ZARIN GOLDBERG

Mary Strittmatter and her husband owned a second home in Ocean City, Maryland, for years. They loved the neighborhood and its location situated along Isle of Wight Bay. Once their two sons graduated college, however, they craved more space, which would allow them to spread out and accommodate the kids and their significant others and friends for weekend visits. The couple was considering another house in the area when a property with direct water views two doors down came on the market.

"It was in rough shape. No one had used the home in years, and it had mold," recalls Strittmatter. "But it is right on the bay, almost like an island—the view isn't blocked by anything, and it was considerably bigger than our old house." Realizing the home's potential, they jumped at the opportunity to purchase it. Retaining the existing footprint, the Strittmatters had the entire home overhauled. "It was originally a very formal, closed-in house that

wasn't oriented to the views," says Strittmatter. An open floor plan was created with abundant windows and doors and more access to the outdoors.

Strittmatter, a design school graduate, brought her friend and former classmate Christie Leu on board to help with the interior design. The home originally had a foyer and living room with ceilings that soared nineteen feet high. In the renovation, the living room ceiling was lowered to accommodate a new bedroom, a bathroom, and a rec room on the second floor. The foyer ceiling, however, remained at the lofty height, which presented a design challenge.

"I start with a home's challenges, so that was my jumping-off point," recalls Leu. "How can I make this high-ceilinged space a focal point?" The solution was to create an accent wall using an ombre paint treatment, where shades of blue fade to white. On the opposite side of the space, paneling adds interest to the wall by the stairwell. Previously, a fireplace took up much of the living room wall facing the ocean view. During the renovation, the fireplace

Instead of a sofa, the porch has a daybed-size swing. The room is easily opened and closed to the outdoors via motorized screens and hurricane storm doors.

was relocated and a sliding-glass NanaWall was installed. The wall opens to a new porch with a day-bed-size swing and an ample bar where the family spends a great deal of time together, enjoying the ocean backdrop.

There's another newly created gathering space upstairs with a comfortable sectional, a large dining table, and a built-in-banquette around a game table. A wall sheathed with navy blue tile complements the banquette's tufted upholstery. "We used the same color palette throughout the house: navy and aqua with warm beige and the occasional pop of pink," says Leu. Strittmatter says creating a cohesive, flexible scheme was deliberate. "We often have a lot of people in the house and things get moved around a lot to accommodate different things. It's great—you can take a chair or a couch out of any room and put it in another space and it looks like it belongs there."

The new house is exactly what the Strittmatters hoped it would be and more. "We even turned the garage into a gym; we are an active family, and friends come by and do circuit training with us," says Strittmatter. "It's so much fun." When the guests have left, though, the home has a peaceful feel to it, she adds, noting that the daybed swing on the porch is her favorite perch to stretch out and take in the ocean view.

OPPOSITE: In the foyer, Christie Leu made one wall a focal point by painting it in ombre shades of blue and white. **ABOVE:** A bar was added to the porch, which blends effortlessly with the living room, enabling the family to entertain large groups.

The foyer opens to the living room, where the fireplace was relocated from its former spot that blocked the view outdoors. Two seating areas were created in the large room to ensure it doesn't feel too big when only a few gather together.

ABOVE: By scaling down the ceiling height, there was space to create a second-story rec room, which has a built-in-banquette seating area. **RIGHT:** The room also has a sizable sectional from which you can view both the ocean and the television.

OPPOSITE: A cozy window seat creates a retreat in the primary bedroom. **ABOVE:** By combining a family room with the existing kitchen, a much larger kitchen was created. An expansive quartz-topped island where guests can converge while the homeowners prepare meals is an integral part of the space.

OPPOSITE: The powder room wallcovering is impervious vinyl. A giant picture depicts a heron, for which the home's street is named. **ABOVE:** The new bunk room upstairs features four cozy bunks fitted with curtains and brass hardware, providing the ultimate sleepover atmosphere.

Its immediate proximity to the ocean makes this home the ultimate seaside escape.

COASTAL COOL

PHOTOGRAPHY BY KARYN MILLET

The first home dwellers in Hermosa Beach towed their tiny suburban cottages to and from the seaside on mule-drawn skids to summer by the sea. Circumstances have evolved considerably since then, but while today you'll find more modern multilevel homes than mini cottages, Hermosa Beach remains unpretentious, relaxed, and unquestionably idyllic. The homeowners of this new retreat, a family with four children, were drawn to this spot for its oceanfront location on the Strand, a long, paved walkway that connects Hermosa to Manhattan and Redondo Beaches.

"It's a great family getaway. You couldn't be any closer to the beach," says Joe Lucas of Lucas Studio, Inc., who created the interior aesthetic for the home: a version of coastal with a contemporary slant. Throughout the three-level home's living spaces, sandy neutrals are paired with ocean tones, and texture abounds.

A travertine fireplace takes center stage in the living room, where the plaster walls are painted a subtle Roman grey. "The room is on the mellow side, so the views take center stage," says Lucas. The kitchen, with its bleached oak cabinetry and grey-and-white herringbone-patterned backsplash, echoes the same vibe. An unrivaled sense of distinction is created with understated details that include counter stools wrapped in seagrass and a brass-trimmed hood over the range.

Bedrooms have a bolder flair, and colors are heightened tones of the blues and greens used elsewhere in the house. In one daughter's bedroom, a wall is sheathed with seafoam-green paneling—a modern nod to the old vernacular of coastal Maine—while another one of the girls has a room with pink grass cloth. In the primary bedroom, Katie Ridder's geometric Scraffito wallpaper emblazons the walls with architectural appeal. A custom chest at the foot of the bed was inspired by a French antique, and the headboard, designed by Lucas, is inset with lacquered vellum.

Lucas felt that the walls along the staircase that runs from the top floor to the bottom level could use

The living room sofa is upholstered in Holland & Sherry outdoor fabric with a terry-cloth-like texture that feels just right for a beach house.

a little pizzazz. "I said to the owners, 'Since everything in the house is on the modern side, why don't we have fun with the stairs?'" Lucas received their stamp of approval and spent the next three months collecting pieces from eBay and vintage shops. The varied collection encompasses "old beachy stuff—paint-by-numbers pieces, old pennants, flags, and nautical elements with a little kitsch," says Lucas of the colorful assortment that frequently encourages travelers on the stairway to take a pause.

The beach room, replete with a pool table, multiple televisions, and a bar, is on the ground level and opens to a sunken patio shrouded slightly from the din of the Strand by a pergola. "It gets a lot of use by the kids, who are teenagers, so the room has a very relaxed feel," says Lucas, who opted for outdoor fabric for the sofa, printed textiles for the chairs, leather upholstered stools, and a jute rug.

"Nothing in the house is too precious," says Lucas. "The owners entertain their friends there, so they wanted it to be a good showpiece for them in some respects. But above all, it's a family house directly on the beach, and they are happy to be able to pop in, wet and sandy from the beach, and not worry about anything other than being together."

OPPOSITE: The living room is anchored by a black titanium (Nero Titanio) tavertine fireplace. **ABOVE:** Seagrass-wrapped stools and bleached white-oak cabinetry lend themselves to the beach environment; pendants are from Visual Comfort.

ABOVE: Eclectic coastal-inspired accents adorn the stairway wall. **OPPOSITE:** The dining room's live-edge walnut-and-bronze table was designed by Lucas; the leather chairs are by Soane.

ABOVE: The lower-level room is a teenager's dream with its pool table and direct access to the beach. The floor's concrete hexagon tiles are visually appealing and indestructible. **OPPOSITE:** A casual outdoor dining table is oriented to take in the activity on the Strand.

A lush mohair rug grounds the primary bedroom, where the views are unrivaled. Lucas designed the chest at the end of the bed, which is based on a French antique.

LEFT: The lower-level bunk room has walls clad with wood and brass ladders that evoke a modern ship. **ABOVE:** An adjacent bathroom is a marvel with its multicolor terra-cotta tile on the walls and floor; the trough sink has three faucets to ensure everyone gets a turn.

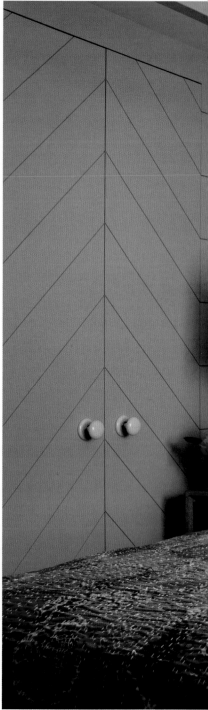

OPPOSITE: For the daughters' bedrooms, Lucas went for a vibe that recalls the eastern coast of Maine and had wood planks installed on the walls and ceilings. This one features a pink grass-cloth wallcovering.
ABOVE: This dreamy space features a charming four-poster bed from Room & Board with an upholstered Kelly Wearstler headboard.

MODERN REVIVAL

PHOTOGRAPHY BY JESSICA GLYNN

In the 1920s, architect Addison Mizner was at the height of his career in Palm Beach, Florida, where the Mediterranean Revival– and Spanish Colonial Revival–style homes he designed were favored by the social elite. Until Mizner's arrival in 1918, when families like the Vanderbilts and Astors were establishing retreats in the area, the buildings of southern Florida were simply pastel versions of the wooden structures found up north. Based on his experiences in Spain and Latin America, Mizner started designing edifices with barrel-tile roofs, stucco walls, and wrought-iron accents; his aesthetic continues to be the preeminent style of architecture in the region today.

When current owners Maxine Gravonsky Gluskin and her husband, Ira Gluskin, first toured this Mizner-designed home one evening, they were struck by the way the residence had retained its original glamour. "There was a magical feeling when we walked in front door," recalls Gravonsky Gluskin. "You could see all the way out to the garden and pool, and it was lit up with candles. There was something very romantic about it."

It was the type of home the couple had been looking for, a refuge from the winters in Canada, where their home base is. The interiors, however, were too dark, with an aesthetic that felt too rooted in the past. "We wanted to brighten the rooms up and make the whole house feel more updated and modern," says Gravonsky Gluskin. "But all of the original decorative elements—the ornate plaster ceilings, the wrought-iron doors and stair rails, the cork flooring in the living and dining rooms—were preserved or repaired."

Since the house has landmark status in the city of Palm Beach, nothing on the exterior could be altered. The preservation work took precision and patience. The intricate exterior tilework was crumbling after nearly a century of salt, wind, and rain. "Our general contractor, Livingston Builders, shipped samples of the tile to a company in Portugal, and they were able to source it in exactly the same pattern and colors," says Gravonsky Gluskin.

New York–based firm Haynes-Roberts Inc. helped reimagine the interiors, a vast project that included resurfacing the walls with marmorino plaster,

The upper level provides a view of the Atlantic on an utterly perfect day.

introducing light and views into the rooms, and sourcing vintage furniture and accessories. Walls are painted stark white or grey-white, and color is introduced only in soft tones, such as seafoam green. The couple entertains friends in the bar, a room that opens to the verdant backyard. Walls are painted a lavender, a trademark that Gravonsky Gluskin says she has included in every home she's lived in.

The furnishings tie into the home's original era and acknowledge the Modernist influences of the 1960s and '70s, particularly in the dramatic, large-scale lighting by renowned designers, including Hans-Agnes Jakobsson. While the home's elements combine to create an air of sophistication that nods to the grandeur of the era in which it was built, there are playful notes, too.

The residence also serves as a backdrop for the homeowners' diverse collection of art. Gravonsky Gluskin is quick to point out that above all, the home is a place for their family—which includes the couple's grown children and grandchildren—to be together, so furniture is comfortable, relaxed in style. "While it is a spacious home, it's not so big you'll get lost in it. It can feel cozy when it's just the two of us here."

"These old Palm Beach houses are just magnificent," says Gravonsky Gluskin. "This is a very solid home that has withstood almost one hundred years of storms and weather and other lives. It's nice to be keeper of the house for a while, and then we will pass it on to someone else who will love it as we do."

OPPOSITE: The home's original colorful tile work reflects architect Addison Mizner's fascination with Venice.
ABOVE: An art piece by Amy Sillman enlivens the bar.

ABOVE: The lilac hue on the bar walls is Benjamin Moore's Balboa Mist; the chandelier was designed by Roberto Giulio Rida. **OPPOSITE:** In the den, where a wall of windows overlooks the garden, vintage furniture—the sofa, by Harvey Probber—is paired with contemporary pieces, including the custom glass-topped coffee table.

OPPOSITE: The stairway off the hallway leads to a tower where Maxine Gravonsky Gluskin has an office.
ABOVE: There is endless fascination in the living room, where the eye is drawn both up to the ornate carved ceiling and down to the graphic composite-and-cork flooring.

ABOVE LEFT: In the breakfast room, the Knoll dining table is arranged under a chandelier by John Salibello. **ABOVE RIGHT:** The crowning elements of the kitchen include the island topped with an ultra-thick slab of Calacatta Gold marble and a La Cornue range. **OPPOSITE:** In the dining room, a custom table is paired with retro Arflex chairs; a butler's pantry is adjacent.

The light-filled primary bedroom's sage green walls and similarly toned custom bed evoke a sense of serenity.

OPPOSITE: An infusion of pink gives this guest room a feminine flair that is accented by the ocean view.
ABOVE LEFT: The primary bathroom is spare and uncluttered, an ideal spot for rejuvenation. **ABOVE RIGHT:** A vintage Bernd Goeckler chandelier provides a pop of vibrant green.

ABOVE: The homeowners spend much time on the loggia, which features an original ornamental ceiling from which a dramatic Foscarini chandelier is hung. **OPPOSITE:** The back, pool-facing side of the home depicts the architect's signature mix of Venetian-, Spanish-, and Southern-inspired styling.

PAST PRESENCE

PHOTOGRAPHY BY JARED KUZIA

Located on Hyannis Harbor, along Cape Cod's Nantucket Sound, Hyannis Port is a small residential village widely known as home to the Kennedy Compound. John F. Kennedy used this coastal haven as a base for his successful 1960 presidential bid and later as a summer White House. Even after six decades, little has changed in the idyllic beachfront enclave. There's a timeless nature to the place, where the shingle-clad houses are kept in the same families for generations. Neighborhood kids learn to sail at the Hyannis Port Yacht Club and participate in beach camp while their parents and grandparents catch up with their summer neighbors.

"Hyannis Port has a real old-fashioned feel," says Shannon Hayden, who has been spending summers in the village since she was a child in the 1970s. "It's a very friendly place, you know everyone. Kids can ride bikes to their friends' houses. We have picnics where several generations gather on the beach. I met my closest friends here during the summer, and we all come back every year with our kids, who are now friends."

Hayden and her husband, along with their teenage children, owned a home in the neighborhood when a place known as the "yellow house" came up for sale. Built in the 1890s, the Victorian home was in rough shape, with vinyl siding, structural problems, and limited opportunities to appreciate the direct ocean views, but the price was reasonable and the Haydens saw the potential to revive it. Richard Curl and Courtney Driver of Curl Simitis Architecture + Design signed on to bring back the home's historic character while adding more vantage points to take in the vista.

"You see some houses and think 'Wow, wouldn't it be great to fix that one up?'" says Curl. "Well, this was one of those houses." The home's original wraparound porch had been closed up and used as a sunroom decades before, so there was no connection to the outside from indoors. By removing the enclosure, it became possible to expose the living room to the ocean view. The new living room has a larger footprint, and can accommodate large groups of people. The original porch posts

A built-in bed nestled between shelves presents a cozy perch to curl up with a good book.

were uncovered and reproduced, and the authentic detailing was restored based on nineteenth-century photos of the house. When the vinyl siding was removed, the team was excited to discover the original shingle pattern, which made it possible to re-create the motif on the top facade of the house, while clapboards were added below.

"With multiple additions over the years, the interior was a mess," says Driver. "We kept all the fireplaces and had the oak floors refinished. We tried to keep as much of the original materials as we could." In other areas of the home, details including window trim and beadboard paneling were created to align with the time period in which the home

was built. Since the six-bedroom house is located in a historic district, the footprint couldn't be altered. Windows, however, were strategically added to enhance views and light. "The second floor felt a bit like a maze," says Driver. "We removed some walls and simplified the floor plan. A new open office/den now serves as a small gathering spot on the second floor for note-writing or sleepovers."

The house is situated prominently on one of only two roads leading into Hyannis Port. "It's one of the first homes you see. There was a lot of buzz going on about it during construction," says Hayden. "People have responded very positively to the renovation. I think they are happy to see it restored."

ABOVE: Furnishings throughout the home feature an array of woven and natural materials with pops of color that vary by room. **OPPOSITE:** Original elements like the carved fireplace surround are paired with beachy modern pieces like this Serena & Lily console table wrapped in raffia.

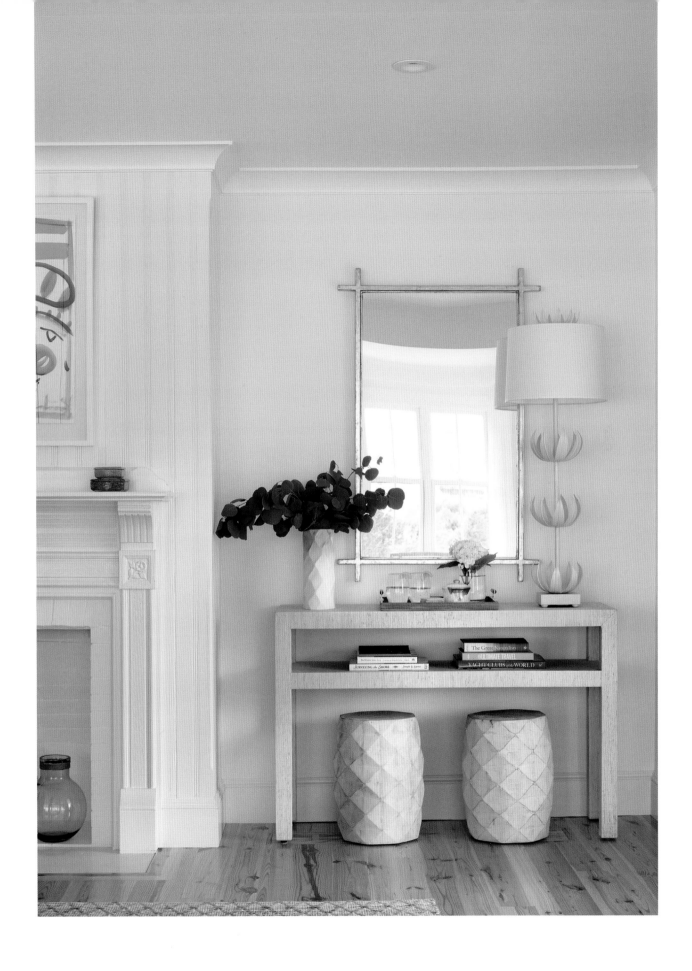

Sheer white drapes frame the window walls on three sides of the living room, ensuring that the ocean is a constant backdrop.

ABOVE: Furniture is comfortable and casual throughout the home; the white sectional in the family room, for example, is slipcovered and can be easily washed. **OPPOSITE:** Various shades of blue, like the deep tone on the mudroom wallcovering, permeate the home.

LEFT: Benjamin Moore's Hale Navy was used on the top portion of the dining room walls, while the lower chair rail is white. **ABOVE:** Framed pleated maps of Martha's Vineyard by Dawn Wolfe hang on the wall.

ABOVE: The kitchen features white cabinetry and a vibrant blue island. **TOP OPPOSITE:** Blue glass tile brightens the backsplash. **BOTTOM OPPOSITE:** A woven rattan bench and chairs from Serena & Lily evoke Parisian bistro styling.

OPPOSITE: In one of the bathrooms, a grass-cloth wallcovering introduces texture that recalls the beach setting. **ABOVE:** Jenny Lind–style twin beds and matching nightstands nestle nicely into a small bedroom with blue beadboard walls.

ABOVE: In another one of the home's six bedrooms, a striking carved wood bed is against a pink accent wall. **OPPOSITE:** Another variation of blue and white is found in a bathroom, where mosaic blue tiles on the floor loosely recall ocean waves.

ABOVE: Since there wasn't enough space in the primary bathroom for a tub, one was installed in an unused porch that was enclosed off the primary bedroom. **RIGHT:** The original floors were refinished but still retain charming imperfections that recall late nineteenth-century cottage architecture.

ABOVE: A small bedroom on the second floor was converted into an office space with built-in shelves and drawers. **TOP OPPOSITE:** The pilasters and columns on the porches were re-created in the original spirit of the architecture. **BOTTOM OPPOSITE:** The front porch had been enclosed for decades. By opening it up, the home was connected to the landscape and ocean beyond once more.

THEMED ATTRACTION

PHOTOGRAPHY BY JANE BEILES

Situated on a tidal estuary that feeds into Long Island Sound, this home in Rowayton, Connecticut, nods to the origins of the unique property: a trolley line that used to transport visitors across the water to an amusement park in the early 1900s. The history and complexity of the site appealed to architect Bruce Beinfield, who purchased the property shortly after it came on the market in 2013.

"The amusement park was a major regional attraction in the 1920s. Big bands like Tommy Dorsey played there," says Beinfield. "There was a roller coaster and many of the park buildings were barnlike structures." The architect's idea was to design a home that evoked the spirit of the park and the character of the old trolley way.

In such close proximity to the water, the site had extensive restrictions. "The house had to be a model of sustainability. I take climate change and sea level rise threats very seriously," says Beinfield. "The structure needed to be environmentally resistant to floods and respect the natural plant and animal life that is part of the estuary."

Designed to be storm and flood resistant, the house sits on twelve concrete piers that enable water to flow under it. Storm shutters protect the glass expanses on the back, water-facing side of the house. Steel support beams ensure the home stands up against high winds. The crisscrosses of lateral bracing on either side of the house reference wooden roller-coaster trestles.

Only sixteen feet across at its widest point, this narrow home features an open floor plan and soaring ceilings. Heavy wood beams in the interior evoke a lodge-like feel, which nods to the site's amusement park history, says Beinfield. Concrete floors on the main level add distinction, especially when combined with the character of the kitchen, where black cabinets and walls offer a sharp contrast to the white cabinet trend which Beinfield has found to dominate homes in coastal locations. Copper was used for the counters and fixtures. "When you put a glass down on copper, it leaves a permanent mark," he says. "I

Salvaged and industrial elements, including a concrete-block fireplace wall, set this home far apart from other coastal homes in Rowayton, Connecticut.

like the idea that every action has a memory and it's constantly changing. Every mark brings more life in the space."

Built-in shelves in the dining room are made of beams salvaged from the shuttered Remington Arms Munitions Factory in Bridgeport, Connecticut. "Bringing historic elements into the space provides more storytelling, more history to the home," says Beinfield, who strives to alter the way ordinary materials are viewed. "We used concrete blocks on a wall in the living room, and it actually has an elegant impact there. Suddenly you're thinking of concrete blocks differently, and your preconceptions about the material are challenged."

Among Beinfield's formulas for creating is establishing a strong sense of order balanced by chaos. He relies on his wife, Carol, an artist, to breathe life into the home through her work—which encompasses various mediums—and her assorted collections, which range from antique dolls to pincushions to painter's palettes. Carol's studio, located on the home's third level, has walls and a steeply pitched ceiling clad with Hungarian wagon-board oak meant to evoke the feel of an old attic.

Beinfield enjoys observing sea life from his attic office overlooking the estuary. From there, he can also see the old shingle cottage that came with the property. In homage to the site's origins, Beinfield commissioned a rail construction company to create tracks connecting the cottage to the main house. The front, street-facing facade of the house is clad with salvaged barn siding. "When people are driving past the house, their first impression is a tall, skinny, quirky barn structure that looks like it might have been there forever," says Beinfield. "I love the idea of the house being a place to be discovered."

ABOVE: An old farm table is paired with mid-century chairs; the pendants above the island are made of concrete. **TOP OPPOSITE:** The exposed ceiling ductwork runs throughout the home's first floor; copper counters are paired with brass hardware. **BOTTOM OPPOSITE:** Pantry shelves are made of Douglas fir with copper piping used as fittings.

The attic studio displays Carol's inspirations, collections, and objects.

In the library, a ladder slides along the floor-to-ceiling bookshelves; Carol's collection of painter's palettes adorns the wall behind the sofa.

ABOVE: Reclaimed boards sheath the ceiling and wall behind the bed in the primary bedroom, which overlooks the tidal estuary. **OPPOSITE:** A guest bedroom features an array of antiques and flea market finds.

ABOVE: The home rests atop concrete piers to allow flood-level waters to flow beneath it. **OPPOSITE:** From the street, the house has the look of a lean, rustic barn.

COLONIAL INFLUENCES

PHOTOGRAPHY BY KARYN MILLET

Surrounded on three sides by the Pacific Ocean's blissful bluffs and beaches, La Jolla emerged as a prime retreat in the 1890s, when a growing rail system first connected this sleepy seaside area to other parts of San Diego. Today, beachfront properties in the area are highly coveted. When a couple seeking a Spanish Colonial–inspired home discovered this haven on a special spot with direct beach access, they knew they'd struck gold.

Interior designer Chris Barrett came on board early, while the architects were still drafting initial plans. His clients—active grandparents with twenty-six grandchildren—had few requirements when it came to décor. "They weren't specific about the look they wanted. Mainly, they wanted a house that would accommodate their family in comfort," says Barrett, who let the coastal locale inform most aesthetic decisions.

At the entrance to the stucco home, which is capped with a terra-cotta tile roof, an elaborate antique-wood door with heavy wrought-iron hardware and a blue-and-white tiled fountain evoke the Spanish Colonial spirit of the structure. Inside, ample windows and doors offer breathtaking ocean views. Earthy, neutral hues with touches of blue-grey are accented by texture and subtle pattern. Throughout the home, antique timber-frame beams and vintage flooring exude a sense of timelessness while infusing modern appeal. "We were looking to give an age and patina to the house," says Barrett. "Older pieces were inserted with new pieces to achieve a collected look."

Each level of the home has access to outdoor space, including a private, man-made beach just off the lower level—which houses a game room for the grandkids, as well as a bunk room and media room. "Since the house is right on the beach, there needed to be a casualness to all spaces," says Barrett. "We wanted to make sure it was very inviting, calm, and luxurious."

When inside, most of the gathering is done in the great room, a large open space that encompasses the living, dining, and kitchen areas. With such a large family, there can be any number of guests at

A casual dining table fits perfectly within a windowed nook in the great room.

mealtime. To accomodate them, Barrett placed an extendable oak dining table—which can seat up to two dozen diners—between the living space and kitchen. Relaxed draperies and upholstery, several made of fabric from Barrett's own line of textiles, add color throughout the home. Lighting provides subtle drama in key spots, including the gold-leaf sunburst in the great room that initially started out as a nineteenth-century wall decoration.

Some elements have Moroccan flair, including the antique majolica tiles and antique sink in the pool bathroom. The kitchen backsplash features another colorful mosaic tile, while the mosaic on the primary bathroom floor is neutral in tone. The tub here is situated in front of long, lean, and arched windows with dozens of colored glass-bottle bottoms fabricated by glass artist Tanya Holroyd Stevenson.

Art paired with graceful architectural detailing provides interest in key areas. In the stair hall, a large blue woven piece picked up by Barrett in a Los Angeles antique shop offers a pleasant juxtaposition to the graceful curved staircase.

The scent of salty air permeates throughout the house, and the beach is the backdrop of nearly every space, especially in the great room. In there, a breakfast table is nestled into a nook of floor-to-ceiling windows. "When you're sitting there, it's just all ocean," says Barrett. "It's truly amazing."

OPPOSITE: An antique door with wrought-iron details nods to the home's Spanish Colonial–style influences.
ABOVE: An olive tree is a central focus of the courtyard where sofas are accented with pillows from Chris Barrett's own textile line.

The furniture is a blend of old and new, says Barrett, noting the freshly upholstered sofa and chair in the family room and an antique side table. The tiles around the fireplace are also vintage.

ABOVE: Beams from Vintage Timberworks line the ceiling of the great room, where the sofas and armchair are upholstered with fabric from Chris Barrett Design. **OPPOSITE:** Above the fireplace hangs a painting by Luc Leestemaker.

ABOVE: A ceiling sheathed with reclaimed wood adds textural interest and an antique vibe. **OPPOSITE:** In the primary bathroom, where the leaded bottle-glass windows are a focal point, the floor tile has a Moroccan flair and marble slabs top the vanities.

A guest room's bed was inspired by an antique iron design; draperies are made of Ferrick Mason fabric.

LEFT: A bunk room designed with the grandkids in mind features bunks with built-in shelves to store favorite bedtime stories. **ABOVE:** The pool bathroom features antique majolica tiles and an antique sink.

ABOVE: The home was designed so each level has access to outdoor spaces. **OPPOSITE:** A double-height window provides a lovely view of the landscape as one descends the sweeping curved stairway.

FAMILY HISTORY

PHOTOGRAPHY BY JULIE SOEFER

The city of Galveston, Texas, is recognized for a lot of things, including its iconic amusement park built on a pier that extends 1,130 feet into the Gulf of Mexico. Rich in character, Galveston's historic districts are lined with Victorian buildings and other architectural marvels that pay homage to the city's heyday as one of the nation's busiest ports.

"Texas can get pretty steamy during the summer months, so it's really wonderful to be able to have an escape to go to in close proximity to the Gulf's breezes," says Mitzi Knust, who, with her husband, has owned a residence in one of Galveston's coastal enclaves for more than three decades. "My husband grew up coming to this neighborhood, and he wanted to share the experience with our children," says Knust of the area on Lake Como, which feeds into West Galveston Bay. "It's a great place for families. Our kids grew up fishing, boating, and waterskiing."

Once the couple's grown children began to have children, they decided a bigger vacation home was necessary. The Knusts were fortunate when a larger house within their golf course community came on the market. "The house has beautiful views of the golf course from the front and the bay at the back. It was the right size, with a pool," says Knust.

To make the house their own, they tapped interior designer Marie Flanigan to reimagine the aesthetic. "The interiors were dark and traditional with ornate yellow and brown tones and Italian-inspired elements," says Flanigan. "It needed a refresh with contemporary detailing."

A mostly white backdrop now permeates through the home, with pops of blue, green, and other subtle natural hues inspired by the surrounding landscape. Various textures, including woven materials and leather, were used to create dimension and interest without detracting from the views, which are intended to take center stage in the house.

"They wanted the home to be a space where they could relax while still having an elevated design sensibility," says Flanigan. "Since there is a lot of activity and kids in the house, we selected a lot of very durable materials and all fabrics are

Woven materials and various natural woods together create a subtle coastal feel.

indoor/outdoor grade."

As of way of adding visual appeal without introducing color, Flanigan clad many of the walls in the home with shiplap, including those in the great room, which encompasses the living, dining, and kitchen spaces. Rather than using boards with a standard eighth of an inch reveal, Flanigan used boards with a quarter of an inch reveal, creating clean lines in keeping with contemporary—rather than historic—styling.

Rustic wood infuses another textural element to the décor. A reclaimed-timber beam serves as the fireplace mantel in the great room, a double-height space with a ceiling that soars nearly thirty feet high. "We had a custom iron light fixture created as a focal point for the space, [which] draws the eye up," says Flanigan.

For rainy days and lazy evenings, a second-floor media room, complete with a coffee bar, is a great place to watch a movie. But most of the time spent at the house is oriented to the outdoors, says Kuntz. "We stay outside most of the day. Since it's so hot here, it's really nice to come inside to a nice cool, neutral palette. The fabrics are nice to touch, and they don't compete with the view the way lots of colorful patterns would." Even when the family is unwinding inside, the absence of window treatments in most rooms allow for prime views of the ocean so they are can feel connected to the outdoors.

"It's a lovely, calming place to be in. Even when we aren't here, we appreciate the house," says Knutz. "Our grandchildren are starting to fish and do the activities that our kids did when they were young. It's special to watch that happen."

ABOVE: A weighty reclaimed beam was repurposed as the fireplace mantle. **OPPOSITE:** Built-in shelves along the stairway showcase an array of beachy accents, including shells collected along the shoreline.

The kitchen counters are made of Neolith, a practically indestructible material.

TOP and **BOTTOM OPPOSITE:** Each of the great room's two seating areas has a lovely—and different—view: One side overlooks the bay, while the other faces the golf course. **ABOVE:** A round table by the window serves as a great place to play cards and other games.

The expanisve great room—which includes the living and dining areas along with the kitchen—feels even larger due to the soaring ceiling that fills the space with abundant natural light.

The media room on the second floor is a great spot to relax and watch a movie; it's even equipped with a coffee bar. An upholstered ottoman is intersected by a rustic wood top that provides a hard surface for drinks and dishes.

ABOVE: A guest room is furnished with a seagrass headboard and a sisal carpet, natural textures that relate to the locale. **OPPOSITE:** White- and grey-washed finishes lend to the primary bedroom's tranquility.

ABOVE: A sitting area in the primary bedroom has a trundle bed where the couple's grandchildren sometimes camp out. **RIGHT:** The four-poster bed is anchored by a simple wood bench with a rush top.

OPPOSITE: The vanity in the primary bathroom is topped with grey-veined faux Calacatta countertops; the floor tile evokes the look of smoky wood planks. **TOP LEFT:** A minimalist shelf hooks into the shiplap paneling. **BOTTOM LEFT:** A mirror framed in driftwood hangs above the tub, which nestles between two walls.

LEFT: A pale grey scheme was used in the guest room, where trunks inspired by vintage steamer trunks sit at the foot of the beds. **ABOVE:** The adjacent bathroom continues the theme with a checkerboard pattern of grey and white floor tiles.

OPPOSITE: Pale blues contribute to the calming vibe in another bedroom. **ABOVE:** The 3,000-square-foot home came with a boat slip and a pool, which ultimately sold the home-owners on the property. **LEFT:** A round mirror in the powder room has a copper patina.

SENSE OF PLACE

PHOTOGRAPHY BY DONNA DOTAN

Situated at the top of one of Nantucket's steepest slopes, this property has a majestic view of Nantucket Harbor and the ocean beyond. Yet when the home-owners began the process of designing their dream retreat, they would learn that working with the topography of this idyllic spot was challeng-ing. Lucky for them, the design team they'd enlisted, Workshop/APD, is well versed in addressing com-plexities and working within the strict parameters of the Nantucket Historical Commission.

"Ultimately, we realized that the best approach would be to utilize the steep site plan to sculpt the home into the landscape and create a series of levels that would highlight the extraordinary view from high to low," says Andrew Kotchen, founding princi-pal of Workshop/APD.

The plan involved integrating an existing historic building with four new gabled structures. "When we do projects on Nantucket, we are big believers in resorting to older forms," says Kotchen, noting that the island's original settlers took the Quakers'

minimalist sensibilities to design. "They used a very simple approach, building gabled boxes with very lit-tle trim and very little embellishment."

In the design of the new home, the top floor of the existing building was removed to create a one-story form consisting of a double-height living room; connected to this part are the three additional gabled forms, each two or three stories high. The facades are sheathed with white cedar shingles and have red cedar–clad roofs so the integrated structures feel authentic in their simplicity and referential to the aesthetic of the region.

"Throughout the property, we worked with a limited material palette of one type of metal, one type of glass, and concrete," says Kotchen. While the exterior feels timeless, even a bit traditional, the interior is more modern. With the exception of those on the home's lower level, every room has a view of the ocean and two to three sides of glass exposure.

Stone was hand split on-site to create a series of retaining walls that make the home nestle into and feel connected to the site. Each of the home's volumes

A slew of textures, including wood, stone, glass, leather, and an animal-hide rug,
are layered to add interest to this seating area.

open to the outdoors seamlessly. When the wide glass doors are completely opened, the boundaries are so blurred it seems the terrace and landscape beyond are extensions of the interior room.

Michael Ellison, Workshop/APD's director of interiors, was tasked with setting the tone for the inside. As the homeowners opted to have all of the walls painted white, Ellison strove to infuse warmth into the rooms with upholstered furnishings, rugs, and layered textures. Wire-brushed oak flooring and natural stone elements anchor the interior to the site, while dramatic lighting provides a contemporary touchpoint. The main living spaces are open to one another, and zones are defined with different material combinations. "When two materials intersect—glass and concrete, for example—it creates an interesting composition," says Kotchen.

There's a theme of combining the old with the new, of merging opposites throughout the décor, says Ellison. The kitchen is dominated by a massive cast volume of black concrete, while the living room is very pale and light. "The rooms are a stark contrast to one another in that way," says Ellison. "There's that balance of light and dark."

The stone above the living-room fireplace goes all the way up to the ceiling. "It's a big swath of grey," says Ellison. "We needed something to break it up." While Ellison was pondering what to get for the spot, the homeowner purchased an abstract painting with shades of green, blue, grey, and tan at a Christie's auction, without having a place for it in mind.

"When I saw how the piece has these colors that are reflected in the landscape outside, I realized it was perfect for that spot on the fireplace stone," says Ellison. "The art bridged the whole room together. That's when you know a project has magic, when something the homeowners are doing coincides with what you do without any discussion."

OPPOSITE: A large-scale painting the homeowners won at a Christie's auction proved to be perfect for the living room. **ABOVE:** The double-height room allows for windows to be accommodated on two levels, which filters even more sunlight into the room.

LEFT: A small loft was created on one side of the living room. **ABOVE:** A swing is poised to observe both the water view through the window and the activity going on in the room below.

OPPOSITE: A lean built-in bar offers a place to eat a quick meal or to work. **ABOVE:** A laid-back hangout space opens up completely to the landscape, blurring any boundary between indoors and outside.

The guest house has direct access to the pool, which overlooks the harbor.

ABOVE: The dining furniture is spare with a live-edge table and leather chairs; the light fixture is made of disks that pool light. **TOP OPPOSITE:** With views on two sides of the room, the ocean is a constant mealtime backdrop. **BOTTOM OPPOSITE:** The weighty island is made of cast concrete.

OPPOSITE: Some of the home's art is nautical, while furnishings nod more subtly to the environment. **ABOVE LEFT:** The stair hall emphasizes the material palette of stone, wood, glass, and steel used throughout the home. **ABOVE RIGHT:** The sculptural glass-encased stairway connects all three levels of the home.

OPPOSITE: Touches of blue give a second-floor bedroom distinction. **TOP** and **BOTTOM LEFT:** Two bunk rooms, where pops of color are more prevalent than the scheme in the rest of the home, accommodate the children in the family and their frequent guests.

ABOVE: A built-in dresser in the primary bedroom was fabricated out of the same wood that accents the peak of the ceiling. **RIGHT:** The zigzag print on the chairs and the bed pillows introduces a little whimsy to a soft, peaceful space.

OPPOSITE: A pergola shades part of the pool deck. **ABOVE:** The home's connected volumes take the forms of the island's earliest architecture; shingle-clad and weathered, the structure feels timeless.

PERSONAL SPACE

PHOTOGRAPHY BY JESSICA GLYNN

During the initial design phase of Kendra Haines's home in Vero Beach, Florida, she told architects Chris Baker and Peter Moor, "I want it to feel like you are on a ship from the inside when you are looking out at the water," she recalls. "That's what they did, from the main room overlooking the porch railing, you don't see anything but the Indian River. I find it so serene and calming."

Prior to building her current home in the area, Haines and her husband had hired Baker and Moor to work on two of their previous homes. Now that their sons were grown, this was going to be a house suited specifically to the couple. "It's an empty-nester house, but with room for the boys when they come to visit," says Haines.

The original house on the property, built in the 1960s, was in poor shape, says Baker. "But it was elevated on the lot and we realized that the house got great views of the river because of the way it was sited. By siting the new home in a similar manner, we were able to achieve that [feeling] of being on a boat."

The house is made up of four connected volumes that are oriented to the river, which flows into the Atlantic Intracoastal Waterway, with gardens and terraces in between. The core of the house is its main room, an open space that is large enough to accommodate the grand piano housed in another room along with fifty guests. "We frequently wheel the piano in and host concerts where local musicians perform. Sometimes we invite students to play or host fundraisers. It's a wonderful place to entertain," say Haines.

And yet the space manages to feel cozy when it's just Haines and her husband. "It's a space that's truly all about us, so it feels comfortable all the time," says Haines. "I love seeing the house with fresh eyes when someone sees it for the first time. Most often they comment on the view."

It's not a fancy house; nothing is too precious by design, says Moor, noting the home's concrete floors. "Floors are always a fussy thing—they can get a lot of wear and damage. The Haineses have dogs and frequent guests. The concrete floors are indestructible.

Every room in the home has a view of the Indian River.

And we added a luster that creates a lovely reflective quality."

Ashley Olivia Waddell and her sister Courtney O'Bryan Whatley collaborated on the interior design of the home. Every room in the house has a view of the river with a slightly different outlook. "My husband loves the view from his office," says Haines, who particularly enjoys the view from the primary bedroom. "The bedrooms are not huge—they are appropriately sized. I wanted them to feel like they belonged in a chic boutique hotel."

Haines is quick to assert that she doesn't enjoy cooking and she didn't need ample prep or storage space, so she uses the wall space in her kitchen to display her extensive collection of artwork. "I said I wanted to have a gallery that happens to have a kitchen in it," she recalls. "I have a collection that I have been working on for forty years. Some pieces I've had since college, others I've found on our travels or are the work of local artists. It's not a valuable collection, but it's all artwork that speaks to me in some way or another." The collection is vibrant and varied, a multidimensional array of paintings, sculpture, textiles, and glass. "The gallery wall pleases me very much. Sometimes I'll look at it and think, 'Oh, this is just as good as looking out at the water.'"

ABOVE: The home office has a doorway large enough to easily move the grand piano through into the living room. **OPPOSITE:** Poured concrete was used for the flooring, which feels cool and smooth underfoot.

The fireplace is built into a wood volume in the living room, which also has storage cabinets and shelving to display books and cherished items.

ABOVE: The absence of a range hood gives the kitchen a less-utilitarian feel, which was intentional.
OPPOSITE: The gallery in the kitchen features art that the homeowners have collected for over forty years.

The first-floor primary bedroom was designed to have the feel of a room in a chic boutique hotel.

ABOVE: Most of the walls and trim are painted white, which contrasts nicely with the polished concrete floors and unique light fixtures. **TOP** and **BOTTOM OPPOSITE:** The home has two courtyards, with the pool on the back coastal-facing side.

SITE SPECTACULAR

PHOTOGRAPHY BY GREG PREMRU

From the street, this home is unassuming: a spare one-story facade topped with a flat roof and clad with cedar siding. Yet as you travel down the long driveway and approach the house, it's evident that the residence, situated on a magnificent piece of land overlooking Buzzards Bay, is much more. "We didn't want the house to appear overwhelming, to be anything showy or grand," says Jeff Goodman, who lives in the house with his wife, Molly. "It's a very private, beautiful site fifty feet above sea level. It was important to know that the house blended in with the land."

The Goodmans, empty nesters, were influenced by the work of Frank Lloyd Wright, Eero Saarinen, and Richard Meier, and they wanted their new retreat to use materials native to the landscape in ways that were different and modern. It was also important that the place have a small carbon footprint. They tapped ZeroEnergy Design to draft plans for the home, led by principal Stephanie Horowitz.

Ultimately, the house Horowitz designed in collaboration with Eleven Interiors is on two levels built on a slope to the water. Great expanses of glass overlook the bay, and multiple outdoor living spaces intersect with the interior. "Floor-to-ceiling sliding-glass doors allow for a really beautiful connection between the indoor living spaces and the outdoor areas, [which] also intersect with the lawn that runs the length of the house and the pool beyond that toward the water," says Horowitz.

The home is very well insulated and air sealed, and because of that, says Horowitz, the team was able to design a much smaller heating and cooling system for the home, resulting in a consistent indoor environment. "All of the primary systems are electric," says Horowitz. "That, in addition to solar panels on the roof, allows the house to produce almost as much energy as it uses."

For the interiors, the major focus, says Michael Ferzoco, principal of Eleven Interiors, was that the scheme didn't interrupt the views of the setting. "Molly and Jeff wanted a clean, contemporary aesthetic. They aren't fans of a lot of accessories," says

The home is oriented to interact with the setting on endless levels.

Ferzoco. "Everything is super functional so the house is able to be used in the very casual way they wanted it to.

"The home truly tells the story of who they are—uncomplicated, successful, generous people—and what they love: contemporary art and furniture in uncluttered, wide-open spaces that can accommodate family and friends in a relaxed, stylized environment," says Ferzoco.

While the house doesn't contain many decorative embellishments, visitors are often awed by the Goodmans' art collection. "We've collected a lot of beautiful pieces over the years, and as we were building the house, we were conscious of where it would be hung," says Molly Goodman. Color was used sparsely throughout, so as not to detract from the pottery, paintings, and sculpture—or from the ocean views.

"The first thing you see when you walk in the front door is a rift-cut oak-paneled wall that stands out," says Gabrielle Bove, lead designer of Eleven Interiors. "We highlighted natural materials in some areas to create attention and focus." A second oak-paneled wall is by the dining room, and the floors feature the same wood but washed to create a lighter appeal. While the scheme centers on a very neutral palette, a few pops of deep blue infuse specific areas—the back of the kitchen island and the dining room built-ins—with bursts of energy.

From the outdoor areas, those pops of blue inside appeal to the eye. "We focused a lot on the outdoor areas, on creating continuity between the indoors and out," says Bove. The efforts of the design team clearly paid off. "The indoor and outdoor spaces merge together so well I'm not sure where one stops and the other begins," says Molly Goodman. "The whole house just has this wonderful flow. If we were to do the project over, I can't think of one thing we'd do differently."

ABOVE: Anchored by a fireplace, a covered porch on the end of the house provides shade and a prime place to take in the view. **OPPOSITE:** The interior side of the black-slate fireplace is in the living room.

The furniture in the home is spare and functional; nothing detracts from the view of the water.

A screened-in porch—with exposed cedar cladding on the doors, windows, and walls—is perfect for dining.

OPPOSITE: With so many windows in the home, accommodating wall-hanging art was a challenge. One solution was affixing art to the back of the floor-to-ceiling wood banks that contain cabinetry and appliances in the kitchen. **ABOVE:** The island was painted blue on the part that faces the outdoor deck so that people sitting there would have something pretty to look at inside.

ABOVE: The same saturated blue found in the kitchen was used on a built-in console in the dining room. The shade, says Pitocco, echoes the ocean and sky. **OPPOSITE:** When not in use, the arms of these low-profile dining table chairs slide snugly under the table.

The living room glass wall opens up completely to the outdoor deck, lawn, and pool, completely obscuring the boundaries between indoors and out.

There is an elevator to the second-floor primary suite so that many years from now the homeowners will be able to age in place.

ABOVE: The home was designed to have both private and communal outdoor spaces, says Jeff Goodman. **TOP OPPOSITE:** All of the outdoor furniture is by Pennoyer Newman. **BOTTOM OPPOSITE:** The upper-level deck has an absolutely unfettered view of the glistening expanse of Buzzards Bay.

RESOURCES

**NANTUCKET HOUSE ANTIQUES
& INTERIOR DESIGN STUDIO**
2 South Beach Street
Nantucket, MA 02554
Nantuckethouse.com

CHRISTIE LEU INTERIORS
9017 Spring Hill Lane
Chevy Chase, MD 20815
Christieleuinteriors.com

LUCAS STUDIO
752 North La Cienega Boulevard
West Hollywood, CA 90069
Lucasstudioinc.com

**CURL SIMITIS
ARCHITECTURE + DESIGN**
533 Main Street, #6
Melrose, MA 02176
Cs-ad.com

BEINFIELD ARCHITECTURE
11 Chestnut Street, #102
South Norwalk, CT 06854
Beinfield.com

CHRIS BARRETT DESIGN
Los Angeles + Palm Desert
Chrisbarrettdesign.com

MARIE FLANIGAN INTERIORS
3201 Allen Parkway, Suite 200
Houston, TX 77019
Marieflanigan.com

WORKSHOP/APD
39 W 38th Street, 7th Floor
New York, NY 10018
Workshopapd.com

**MOOR, BAKER & ASSOCIATES
ARCHITECTS**
2928 Cardinal Drive
Vero Beach, FL 32963
Moorarch.com

ELEVEN INTERIORS
535 Albany Street
Boston, MA 02118
Eleveninteriors.com

ZEROENERGY DESIGN
156 Milk Street, Suite 3
Boston, MA 02109
Zeroenergy.com

ACKNOWLEDGMENTS

Much gratitude goes to my first editor at Gibbs Smith for this book, Katie Killebrew, who accepted my proposal back in 2020, early on in the pandemic, when I was desperately dreaming of brighter days. Scouting homes by the ocean—mostly from a computer screen—was indeed an optimistic pursuit that contributed to the rejuvenation of my soul during that bleak spring and uncertain summer.

When Katie moved on to a new venture, Sadie Lowry then took the reins, helping to guide and shape my manuscript. Yet for a book of this sort, words are nothing without images. And it is to the photographers—Jane Beiles, Donna Dotan, Jessica Glynn, Stacy Zarin Goldberg, Jared Kuzia, Karyn Millet, Greg Premru, and Julie Soefer—who captured the homes featured on these pages to whom I am most grateful. Your images made this book the lovely volume that it is.

To all the owners who permitted me to peer into their cherished havens, let me ask questions about them, and showcase them for the world to see, thank you for being so welcoming.

And in my own family's special retreat by the sea—which is located not on the ocean, but just down the street from it—thank you to Mike, once again, for holding down the fort while I met my deadlines: you are my star.